T0113543

RAJ GUPTA III

EARNING SIX FIGURES IN CORPORATE AMERICA

WITHOUT A DEGREE

authorHOUSE

AuthorHouse™
1663 Liberty Drive
Bloomington, IN 47403
www.authorhouse.com
Phone: 833-262-8899

Published by AuthorHouse 09/09/2020

ISBN: 978-1-7283-7287-7 (sc)
ISBN: 978-1-7283-7286-0 (e)

Library of Congress Control Number: 2020916903

Print information available on the last page.

This book is dedicated to God, the one who has given me strength and wisdom, to my three beautiful children, and to my late great grandmother Ja'net Dubios. They are my motivation to keep growing and to be a better person day after day.

CONTENTS

INTRODUCTION

My name is Raj Gupta III. I am twenty-nine years-old and have worked ever since I was seventeen years old when I had to drop out of high school to provide for myself and for my young daughter.

I was always ambitious and wanted to keep reaching for new levels of accomplishment. After dropping out, I started applying to different odd jobs, and I stumbled upon a Kirby vacuum franchise. I called in for an interview and I got it, I showed up the next day but I didn't have a resume to give them. I told the recruiter that I was seventeen and I had a newborn. I also told him that I planned to be a millionaire by the time I turn thirty. The recruiter laughed at me and said they didn't have a position for me. As he was walking me towards the door, I asked, "Is there is nothing I can do?" Before I left, I took the recruiter's name and told him that he would be hearing from me. And he did. I called four times that day asking to speak with him. He finally took my call and said, "You're more persistent than most people who work here, so your training starts on Tuesday. Be here at 9 a.m."

I was so overwhelmed with joy that I forgot how hungry I was and how I needed money to buy food for the week. The mother of my first born was an angel and did the shopping for food that day in celebration of my new job. Her family had taken me in because, despite the fact that I had nothing to offer, they saw that I was putting in the effort to be there and provide for my young family. This is a public thank you to the Johnson Family.

I was wearing my new oversized goodwill clothes when Tuesday came. Though the recruiter had said that my training would begin at 9 a.m., I was at the office at 8 a.m. Even sitting alone in the training room for an hour couldn't wipe the smile from my face. I felt like I had won an important battle, not realizing it was only the beginning of my fight.

The training manager was an energetic girl who was extremely passionate about her job. There were about thirty people in my training class, and I was the youngest person there by quite a few years. I began to overthink everything, my heart was racing at a mile a minute, and I began to sweat.

Three days later, my training was complete. Despite what I had learned, I felt completely overwhelmed. I had no idea what my job title or responsibilities were. I had no idea what I was expected do. I was completely lost.

The first day of work

The night before my first day, I was so overwhelmed I couldn't sleep at all. I had been given all these materials and training packets, and I spent the whole night studying sales scripts and price sheets and financing options. It was only then that it dawned on me that I was going to be selling something in my new position. I didn't know if people were going to come into the store, and if they didn't, I didn't get how we would find customers.

Despite my lack of sleep and uncertainty around what was expected of me, I was ready for a challenge that first morning. When I got to the office, I went to a large meeting room where about seventy-five to eighty people of all ages and from all walks of life were waiting. At the appointed time, someone turned off the lights and started blasting music; the people around me started high-fiving one another and jumping around. I felt like I joined a cult and running away.

It shocked me that people were having so much fun at work. To see such laughter and joy in a space usually associated in my mind with drudgery was a beautiful and rare experience. I tried to take it all in and just enjoy seeing such energy in people from such different cultures, economic backgrounds, and of such varying ages. I was so inspired by their energy that somehow all my fear just washed away.

After the music died down, we sat for a thirty minute meeting to help prepare us for the day ahead as well as to celebrate al the deals the sales team closed over the weekend. I did some basic math in my head and, based off the number of sales just the previous weekend, I was convinced that the owner of the company had to be a millionaire. I decided right then and there that I needed to meet him. Though I had joined the company with no ambition greater than making enough money to pay my bills and provide for my daughter, after that meeting I began to think bigger. I began to ask: how can I build something like this?

After the meeting ended, I jumped into a van with seven other people and we drove off. In the van, they handed me flyers and told me that I would be going door-to-door to make my sales pitch. They told me exactly what they expected me to say and, five minutes later, the person driving the van—who I learned on the drive was my manager for the day—pulled over and told me to get out. He instructed me to knock on every house door on the street call him if anyone said they wanted to take a look at a demonstration.

I began to feel anxious as I approached my first door.

I had at least 120 people say no to me that day and not one person gave me an opportunity to give them a demonstration no matter how hard I smiled. I really wanted to show them just how impressive the Kirby vacuum was, but not one of them would give me that opportunity. It was an inauspicious start to my first day at a new job.

I knocked from about twelve in the afternoon until around nine o'clock. When I finally made it home that night, I could barely move my legs. I was drained, and I didn't say a word to anyone; I just went straight to the bedroom and threw myself onto the bed. I was so beat up emotionally, mentally and physically. Most of the other new employees that started with me said they weren't coming back the next day because they'd rather work at McDonalds than knock on doors every day. At that moment, laying down on my bed, my body was in complete agreement, but then I remembered how hard I had pushed to get the job, and I didn't want to let anything push me down.

Looking down at my daughter's face the next morning, I said to myself: *I am going to make this job work. I am going to fight for this life.* I had butterflies in my stomach again when I jumped on the team van for my second day of work, but it was a quiet storm of butterflies. As we drove to the street we would be working that day, I keep saying to myself: *I am going to make it. I will be successful. I will do it.*

I knocked on doors for three hours and was rejected again and again. When I got to the last door on the street, I called my supervisor to let him know I was completed with my area. I knocked on the last door, it opened, and I was greeted with a warm smile and a friendly "What are you selling?"

I laughed and said, "I am selling $2,500 vacuum cleaners; you want to buy one?"

"Absolutely not!" she exclaimed in response.

"Look," I said, "before you make up your mind, let me at least show you what it can do. I'll be right back."

She smiled and laughed at my audacity. I took action before she could change her mind grabbed my stuff from the team van and walked back to her house. Once inside, I had trouble putting the vacuum together. It took me at least twenty minutes to get it put together and in good working order. She laughed at historically inept fumbling the whole time. When I finally was able to show her how the Kirby worked, she could see immediately how impressive a piece of technology it really was. She loved the features, and it was clear that, despite the high price, she wanted one for her home.

"If I could save you money off the list price, would you consider buying one today?" I asked her.

"No." she responded. "I don't have $2,500 to spend on a vacuum cleaner right now."

"I completely understand," I said. "It's a lot of money to spend on a vacuum."

But, then she surprised me and asked, "Do you accept credit cards?"

"Every single one," I replied, pulling out a contract.

In that moment, I experienced a level of joy that I have never been able to replicate. It had something to do with overcoming an obstacle that made so many other people give up or quit. It also had to do with accomplishing something that, up until the very moment it happened, I had thought was impossible. Though I was never able to fully replicate the feeling of that first sale, I used the motivation I got from that first successful sale to push on and try harder and harder everyday. Would it surprise you to learn that I soon became one of the top Kirby sales representatives in the country? That I later lead a sales team of my own? That I eventually opened my own Kirby franchise where I trained my own sales team and made over six figures selling Kirby vacuums over a period of five years?

After settling down and starting a family, I sold off my franchise as things started to slow down. It was a different time having so much freedom and me being used to working 18 hour days. I then took on management roles in the merchant services, solar, and digital marketing industries. After years of hard work and dedication, I am now the owner and CEO of my own marketing firm. My path has not been linear, and I have gotten to where I am today through much trial and error, and many ups and downs. Though I have had many successes in my career, I have also had ventures that ended in failure and incurred significant financial losses. I wouldn't change one step in my journey because it was that journey—with all its mistakes, missteps, and failures—that made me so strong that when issues arise now I can handle them with grace. I no longer fear rejection; I see it for what it really is—a small setback in a greater path to success. I move at a pace, and I believe—no, I know—that all dreams are possible.

I decided to write this book to share some of the Key Principles that allowed me, a high school dropout and sixteen-year-old father with limited opportunities, to overcome the odds and become successful. I have used these Key Principles to make it in corporate America. While I will take credit for organizing and systematizing these Key Principles in this book, I am really just the messenger, for much of what I present here I learned from watching and talking to people who were successful. Observing what worked for them and adapting it to my own situation is how I became successful, and how I developed the Key Principles I will share with you now. In addition to learning the skills, techniques, approaches, and mindset of successful people, I also took the time for self-improvement, meditation, and prayer. Time with God has been an instrumental part of my success and my overall well-being. My mentors, my faith, and my family have instilled in me the value of giving back, of making sure other people have the opportunity to change their lives for the better.

Before I start enumerating my Key Principles, I want to issue a quick, but important, warning: this book is not for people who want to pull down a six-figure salary without putting in the necessary work. Firstly, earning six figures at anything these days simply means you're average. Making over $100,000 a year for the first time is a big deal—it certainly was for me when I had my first $100,000 year at the age of twenty-four. However, most people stop at that first $100,000. Instead of pushing through to new levels, they get comfortable with their island vacations, their trips to Las Vegas, and the Mercedes-Benz and Audis in their driveways. They get caught up in the endless cycle of purchase and payment, buying an endless assortment of commodities with no real value, so that when they are presented with a real opportunity to invest in something of value most of them don't have much to invest with.

If you do any research—or even a simple Google search—you will find that only five percent of Americans earn over $250,000 per year. That that only twenty percent of the six-figure earners make multiple six figures per year incomes. The folks who earn $250,000 or more are the ones who kept pushing when others got comfortable. In order to grow—financially, personally, spiritually—you have to get uncomfortable. There were three times in my life when I felt particularly uncomfortable, and those are the times when I pushed myself and grew the most. The first time I experienced this level of discomfort was when I was a new father at sixteen having to buy diapers and formula for my child but I no job with which to earn the money I needed to do so. The second time, I was seventeen and briefly homeless, despite having a job that I was working hard at. The time I was the most uncomfortable was when I was twenty-eight and my wife took the kids and left me because of my infidelity.

Each one of these times in my life was one from which I was able to grow. I think what I learned from these experiences is how to be comfortable with being uncomfortable. As importantly, I learned that my present isn't my future and my past isn't my present. That is, who I was—a sixteen year-old high school dropout or a homeless seventeen year-old kid—doesn't determine who I am now; and who I am now won't necessarily determine who I can become in the future—that if there is discomfort in the present, I will overcome it. When life became difficult—and, trust me, it did—this outlook allowed me to become my own inspiration. I found a way to hold on to that future knowing that I would be able to breathe life into the things that felt dead in my life. I knew that things wouldn't change overnight, that I needed to keep moving forward on the journey of my life and change things slowly, one step at a time; one moment at a time.

I have learned that the thing that really bring me to a place of happiness in life is waking up and realizing that I have accomplished what I set out to do. I want to share with you an exercise that I used to help me in my journey: take a moment to write out what you want your future to look like in three years, five years, and ten years' time. Write down the vacations you want to take, the house you want to buy, the job you want to have. Once you have all that down on paper, read through it and visualize yourself taking that vacation or buying that house; see yourself receiving that award or paying for your child's first semester of college. Visualize all the things you want to accomplish. Now take the final and most important step and write out all the little things you can do each day to make you more effective, more productive, and more effective at your job—all the little things that will bring you closer, day-by-day, to achieving your goals.

If you go back to Google one more time, you'll find that only one percent of Americans earns more than $1,000,000 per year. That means only twenty percent of the Americans making over $250,000—already only five percent of all Americans—go on to earn seven figures. How to become part of that fraction of a fraction of all Americans—how to make the money you truly dream about making—starts with mastering the things you *do* have control over. Pay your bills, and pay them on time. Make wise investments, and, if things don't work out with one investment, don't let that stop you. Keep going! If you work hard and are smart with your money, you will have success. Don't let life's many distractions pull you away from what you want out of life. When I was younger, I spent my money on renting limos, getting table service when I went to the club—basically spending way more money than I needed to, money that could have been invested. I realized the error of my ways, but my education was a painful and expensive one. I don't want you to make the same mistakes that I made, the mistakes that could have derailed my career and my life. In this book, I will breakdown how you can learn from your mistakes in order to stay focused and continue growing your wealth.

I think it's important to know that this book is focused on giving you the Key Principles to make six figures *every* year. Anyone can do pretty much anything once. This book is focused on consistency. I think one gift that God has given me is a respect for and a love of work. I wasn't always the smartest person in the room, nor was I the fastest learner or the quickest thinker, but no one no one could out-work me. I wasn't scared of working after hours or before work. I made myself available at all times for clients or customers. It helped me rise to the top in every situation.

You will need to learn to always move forward and try to progress. If you're reading this and think you're working hard already, well guess what? With all due respect, you're not. There is always something more that you can do. There is always room for improvement somewhere— whether that be in how you talk to your customers or how you deal with the frustrations of not being where you want to be in life. Take the time to write down the areas you can improve on in your daily life and make note of the places where you are falling short. Figuring out what you can work on—and then putting in the work to improve—will set you on a path to success.

Earning $100,000 per year means making $383 per working day (excluding weekends). Why am I telling you this? Because, if you must *know the numbers!* You can't measure where you are going—and how close you are to that goal—without knowing the numbers. It doesn't matter if you sell Avon or Amway or newspaper subscriptions, you need to know how many people you need to sell your product or services to in order make the amount of money you wish to make. It's impossible to hit a target you have. Too many people just wake up in the morning and just go to work without a clear sense of why they are doing it. A successful person needs a goal and a roadmap of the steps necessary to accomplish it.

This book is a simple guide to what I did to earn six figures in corporate America without a college degree, working my way up from sales rep to manager to director and now to owner and CEO. But—and here is my warning—these Key Principles don't "work" on their own, they require their follower to work hard, show discipline, and stay focused.

THE ART OF
BEING PATIENT

If you think you're just going to jump into a new job at a new company and start making millions of dollars immediately, think again. For most people, no matter the position they start in, it takes at least six months of hard work, rejection, and failure before they start to see positive results. In order to be successful, you need to be patient and learn everything you can during your first few frustrating months on the job. I like to think of jobs the way people think of relationships, and I refer to this initial feeling-out period as the "Ninety Day Rule." Just as how you don't always feels the same way about a person you are in a relationship with after ninety days, you might not feel that you are a good fit for your company—or that your company isn't a good fit for you—after that same amount of time. If your first ninety days at a new job have been filled with turmoil, then I would suggest you start looking for another job. *You* are in control of your destiny and *you* have the ability to work in America in any capacity—whether that be in a call center for a small sales organization or as an executive for a Fortune 500 company—no matter your race, your creed or your color.

Will there be obstacles because you may not have the requisite certification or degree? Yes! Will there be discrimination, racism, and favoritism in the workplace? Yes! But that's what makes life interesting—writing the great story for your life!

I have realized over my life and career that you can't change someone's views, but you can change their viewpoint. I worked and reported directly to the CEO of a company and he wasn't a very easy person to deal with he would expect for everyone to love and almost worship him for the opportunity he provided the expectations for him at least was to "milk everyone for all you can" I think that mentality is overrated because people aren't cattle, People need to be built up and can be trained and learn new things. Before I left this company not only did I hire a new guy that everyone felt would be impossible to train the person who was promoted into my roll he wanted to fire and the top sales rep was the kid that the CEO had an a negative opinion of both people that steeped up when I parted ways were different when he saw their true potential like I did in the beginning, see people for who they are at first not who they are in the middle or the end. But as humans we operate in current circumstances without all the facts and we tend to jump to conclusions at times on people or what we think but the view point can change over time. So if your boss hates you or the company has an opinion change the narrative change the view point. I also changed a view point I worked for a company were based on my writing skills I will be the first to tell you it was less than perfect and I struggled putting emails together but I was great at selling over the phone so I was able to make up were I lacked in other areas to do well at that job inter enough the company asked that I would take tutoring to help with the writing skills. I was completely embarrassed at first and felt singled out and not open to the idea although it felt rather forced can I tell you that after six weeks I did start to see an improvement and help me with my grammar and writing skills my view point changed. Whether someone's opinions or views are accurate or not, you can't let it affect who you are as a person and how you see yourself and your potential. So many times, we respond to disappointment, frustration, and set-backs emotionally, but that kind of response—especially in the workplace—shows weakness, and you can't allow yourself to have big emotional displays if you want to advance professionally. You need to master your emotions and focus on being a consummate professional, never losing sight of the task at hand and what you are trying to accomplish. That it no way means you should ever tolerate disrespect or discrimination, but it does mean you should always try to handle it professionally—through the proper channels with HR. Don't be afraid to take a stand, just make sure it's for the right reasons. Taking a stand!!!! Take the right action when need it's ok to think things through pause sit in silence these things help make putting a process of people in place to be a sounding board. My grandmother would always say there is a multitude of safety in concial. Don't be afraid to let the people who think similar to how you do hear your ideas. Make sure they share with your ideas the same way they do as well. If you're not being treated fairly in your day to day job or workplace see first if there is a possibility to change the narrative do everything you can if that doesn't work then change your environment find a new place first know your value and what you bring to the workplace. Your next question is well Raj How do I know my value? When you wake up get out of bed and your ready to take on your task for the day then you have value how much of it transalutes to how much money you bring to the company or how much money you can save either way your value is always going to due with a number equaling money.

One of the ways that I was able to accomplish so much was through setting goals. In the next section of this book, I want to talk you through how I was able to reach so many milestones—financial, work, and personal—through setting goals for myself.

Principle One: Setting Goals

Most people believe that they already do set goals for themselves—and they might—but I want to share with you the steps I take to successfully set goals for myself. These techniques have worked for me, and I know that they can work for anybody—even you!

The first step I take is to write down my goals. So many people set a goal in their head for what they want to do or accomplish but then lose sight of what that goal was when the realities of their present life—paying the rent, buying groceries, maintaining relationships—take their attention away their dreams for their future. The simple act of writing your goal down is a powerful one. It takes that goal out of your head and makes it "real" in world. Moreover, it is harder to forget what it was when it is written down right there in front of you!

Second, I make sure that the goals that I set for myself are realistic ones based on what I am looking to accomplish. For example, you can't expect to make a million dollars at a company that generates $250,000 a month in revenue—that is not a realistic expectation. Let's look at a salesman or saleswoman that makes $150,000 per year and try to understand how they do it in order to reverse-engineer what our goals—should we want to make that same salary—should be. Looking at how their work breaks down, we see that our hypothetical salesperson makes 5,000 sales calls a month and generates $9,800 in sales. That work, added to their hourly salary, brings their annual income up to $150,000. So, if you want to take home the same salary, then you need to set your goals around hitting the same targets. That is a plan, and it is based on data.

As important as having data and targets is, you also need to make room—emotionally and psychologically—to fail. Even if your goals are based on strong data points and are realistically achievable, there is no guarantee that you will hit them the first time out. You must allow yourself to fail, to learn from that failure, and to grow comfortable with being uncomfortable. You have to jump, even if you sometimes fall and get hurt. That is the only way you will learn.

The reason why data and goals are so important is that

you can't understand your worth without them. Without knowing your worth, you won't know how much you need to strive to make every day—you will be fighting like hell, but you won't know what you are fighting for! One way to make sure you give yourself the best opportunity to reach your goals is to know your commission or bonus plan in detail. With that knowledge in hand, write out five or six different ways you could make $8,333— the pretax amount you need to make monthly in order to have an annual salary of $100,000.

Let's look at another example: if you sell shoes online, write out how many shoes you need to sell in order to make $8333 in profit after expenses. The same principle applies regardless of whether you sell makeup, sell clothes, offer accounting services, or work in any kind of sales-based business or industry. Figuring out *your* numbers is key.

If, however, you can't get to your number for whatever reason despite your best efforts, then you may need to start looking for another position or opportunity. Don't hold yourself back and don't be afraid to try new things—even new jobs in new and different industries. It is on you to take whatever action is necessary to find the right opportunity for yourself. Even once you have found where you need to be, all types of things will pop up and try to deter you, and there will still be all kinds of problems you will need to overcome—so be prepared. I say this not to discourage you, but so you can be in the best possible position to handle them when they do come up.

Principle Two: Play Hurt

So many times, life just kind of happens—even more so when you have a spouse, children, and other family that depend on you—and can lead to an immense feeling of pressure and mental blocks that make it hard to focus on your work and career. Even if you are young, single, and just starting out, you could have struggles of your own. After all, starting out on your own in the world can be a lonely and isolating experience. Regardless of your age or status, we all live in a world where things that happen within a seconds can change our lives forever in a negative or a positive way. When those negative things happen, do you just quit and stay in bed all day? Do you cry? Do you go out drinking, smoke weed, or do coke to numb the pain and hurt?

You may do some or even all of those things—but you shouldn't, not if you want to be successful. If you want to achieve your goals, I have some advice for you: go to work!

Get up and play hurt. This life is going to keep giving you this same lesson until you truly understand what it takes to master your ability, figure out what your mission truly is, and set yourself on the path to get there. You can overcome any and all hardships as long as you believe you can and aren't afraid to play hurt. You need to believe in yourself and keep moving toward your goals—don't let anything stop you ever no matter what the situation is.

I will give you an example from my own life to help illustrate this Key Principle. Back when I was the sales director at a company, I was given a very big project for which I was expected to find a certain amount of buyers and sellers within a thirty-day time frame for a business idea I had come up with. The pressure was really on me because in addition to all the responsibility I had on this project, I was still managing a team of 6 people a few of them where new and others had been around for a while but I felt like I was always grabbed to put fires out. Two weeks into my thirty day window I still had no buyers or sellers I was failing tremendously, and I had probably made over 200 calls a day to try to reach my goal. At the same time, my wife and I were going through a difficult patch, I had family members in need, and I felt like my whole world was crashing down on me all at once. I ended up getting really sick from the stress of it all and I remember having many sleepless nights during this difficult period. With only seven days to meet my deadline I was miles away from hitting my goals. But I went into the office every day and never stopped trying. Low and behold somehow, after three successful days in a row of making a few things happen, I was able to bring in the business I needed to and meet my goals. Everything just came together and, all of a sudden, I was a hero at the office. I felt amazing almost unstoppable for a little bit. It's like winning a race that you train 6 months out of the year like winning the superbowl and winning the finals in the NBA. No one can ever take those moments away from you own that and grow through that and you have clarity that you can accomplish more through difficult times. If you're reading this book understand that no one but your opion of you matters.

The lesson I took from this experience was that no matter how badly the month started and was continued to go, I still showed up every day regardless of what was happening in my life. Regardless of the sleepless nights. Regardless of the difficult situation at home. I kept showing up because it was my obligation to set a goal see it through. I was hurt and hurting—but I played through the pain to hit my goal.

Principle Three: Face all Fears

All of us have things that holds us back mentally—whether they be episodes from our childhood that we hold onto or insecurities about our intelligence or capability to do our job well. What I have learned to do to manage the things that once held me back is to take a few deep breaths when I wake up and repeat a very simple mantra to myself: *This will be the greatest day of my life no matter what comes my way I will be successful and I will overcome.* And, at the end of each day, I like to think about what I have accomplished that day—whether that be reading a book, learning how to build something, or just using my imagination. These little things can have a big effect. I do these things because I used to wake up and say to myself "well what's going to happen today? Better yet I would check social media and see how great other people's life's are and focus on what other people are doing? I would even watch the news to hear about all other current events. I realize after doing all of these things it brought other peoples problem concerns or issues into my world. When you wake up it is the most important part of your day and sets the presence for the rest of the day.

To make six figures and more consistently, it takes discipline, consistency, patience, and a basic understanding of numbers. You need to continue to craft your skills to always be better, and part of becoming better means overcoming your fears. Here is an exercise that you can do to help you deal with fear:

> *Focus your mind on your three biggest fears. Close your eyes and take three deep breaths. Then say to those fear, "you no longer exist." Let your self-doubt fade away. Try to hold onto a real understanding of this simple truth: that everyone came into this earth the same way, and everyone will leave the same way.*

You can do anything you set your mind to. The problem is we lose sight of that fact when we get hurt by people or when we feel that God didn't answer our prayers. We lose sight of our own power and potential when things don't work out the way we want them to. But, you need to remind yourself—sometimes you will need to remind yourself a lot—that you really can accomplish anything—and I am living proof. I have been able to overcome every obstacle that has been placed in my path. Why? Because I am smarter than everyone else? No. Because I worked harder than everyone else? Not really. I have been able to succeed because I figured out that someone else's opinion isn't my reality. What that means is that regardless of what you or anyone else thinks about me, regardless of the mistakes I have made and will continue to make, I am here to live life abundantly. You can do the same. Start by allowing yourself to own those words, then allow yourself to own your success. You have dreams and goals for a reason—to live them out.

Principle Four: Get Used to Failure

Failure is in itself an invigorating experience. Building a successful career isn't easy, and building a successful business is even harder. Most people in my generation haven't experienced much rejection. We have grown up at a time when everyone gets a trophy. To far too great an extent, we have been "bubble wrapped" to protect us from failure. And yet, failure is almost always a part of every career path. However, I believe that Millennials—of which I am one—want to live the good life that our parents and grandparents achieved *over time, and we* want it *now.* The way I always explain this to people is through the metaphor of cooking: my generation is accustomed to the ease and immediacy of the microwave, but our parents are used to the longer time it takes to properly *cook* their food. Their food may take longer and require more effort, but it also tastes better! I have realized over time that when we rush things—whether that be food or our own path to success—we lose something important in the process.

I love the word *earn*, which means to come to be duly worthy of or entitled to or suited to. I understand that definition as saying you earn something through effort and power of will. And to me, will power comes from failure. I think you are foolish if you think that any long-term successful business won't encounter some kind of failure. It will happen. What matters isn't that you fail, it's how you prepare for that failure that will make you successful. How do I prepare for failure? There is no preparation for failure you have to begin to expect its part of your journey. Also understand it's going to happen, the more competerable you get with expecting that feeling the better off you will be.

People think I am insane when I say this, but you need to celebrate your problems, no matter how big or small, not run from them. There is a lesson in adversity and failure, but it's up to you to learn that lesson and grow from it. Once you have faced a certain kind of adversity or problem, then it can no longer affect you the same way because you will have learned how to move past it.

Principle Four: Picture Perfection

For this Key Principle, imagine your brain is a camera that can take perfect pictures and videos of every image that plays out in your mind's eye. Now, take five to ten minutes (and try to do this at least three days a week) to envision what a successful life looks like. What does your future home look like? Your cars? Your family? Create an entire world in your mind. What type of vacation do you want to take? Don't hold back: let your thoughts run wild. Now, with that mental camera of yours, take a video of these moments and store it in your mental memory.

DREAMING DURING THE DAY

Some of the greatest things in the world are worth waiting—especially because you will value achieving them even more if you have really had to wait and work for them. One of the best ways to bridge the gap between the wanting and the achieving is through visualization.

The art of visualizing what is important to you is something that you do this while at home or in the car— or even at work. All you need to do is close your eyes and see—"visualize"— yourself receiving that $10,000 commission check or that hefty bonus. I used to close my eyes and visualize filling out my taxes on a six-figure salary! What I would do during a stressful day is go and take a walk and think about the life I saw for myself not the battels that I was dealing with at the present time. Dreaming during the day is an exercise that should be done alone between yourself and thinking about the future you see for yourself the things that you want to bring into reality. I suggest doing this for at least 10 mins daily or an hour weekly can do it. This process will help you bring things that are important to you to present circumstances.

Principle Four: Where Do You See Yourself

Visualize where you want to be and make sure your mental image is as detailed as you possibly can make it. This isn't an exercise in generalizations, this is an exercise in which you should picture exactly what you want—down to the smallest detail. At the age of eighteen, I was sleeping on a floor in a rented room of a disgusting home, and when I say disgusting I mean you could catch a disease by touching the door handle to the bathroom. For that squalid room, I paid $350 a month. I had nothing. No bed. Very few clothes or other possessions. What I did have was a dream—and a relationship with someone who wanted to share that dream with me. I had so many visions of owning my own home and buying new cars and traveling the world. There was nothing in my life that would have suggested any of this would be possible for me, but I had the dream and willingness to work to make my dreams come true.

Though there were times when doubt would slip in after a difficult day or when life just became so incredibly overwhelming, I always had a place to go where I could remind myself of how great my life was going to be. For me, that place was the beach—far away from my empty room— where I felt peace and love. The beach was special to me, and I wouldn't share the space with anyone, not even my partner. As I walked through the sand and listen to the waves lapping against the shore, I would regain my belief in myself and become stronger. It became my meditation before I even understood what that word meant.

I encourage you to find a place—whether it's a rooftop overlooking the city or a mountain top or a calm park or placid lake—where you can have time to yourself to just dream. If you share this space with someone make sure it's someone who is extremely special and shares your dreams for the future.

Principle Five: Feel your way into your Dreams

What does success mean to you? What will it feel like when you buy your dream home? What does it feel like to travel the world? What does it feel like to be financially stable? What does it feel like when you hit your sales goal? Do you know what any of these moments feels like? If the answer is no, then you really aren't close to your achieving your goals or living your dream life. I have that "feeling" my way to success has been a very effective strategy. What does that mean? It means that I strive to "feel" what it will be like to experience an event—usually a positive one—in my future.

Whatever your vision of success is, find it and think about it when things get tough at work or at home. When you are struggling, you need to "see" and "feel" the joy of you signing up that big client. Focusing on that feeling—rather than the difficulties of the moment—will give you clarity of purpose and help re-focus your attention on your goals. before it happens feel what the moment will feel like when you close that major deal.

Principle Six: Find *Your* Space

Understand that finding your space could be a quite office your living room your closet anywhere doesn't have to be outside the home but it can be as long as you can be conf and find your thoughts. Right now, you are on a path towards achieving everything you have ever wanted in life—but that can only happen if you continue to move in that direction. One way to stay focused is to find your space, the place where you feel most relaxed. Once you have found it, you need to hold onto that space, and be present there with no distractions. Most people tend to focus on what they don't have or what they don't want in life more than the things they do want. When you are in *your* space, focus on the good things in your life that you can see, focus on love you feel each day, and focus on bringing all your most important dreams into the world. If you can make this a daily or weekly practice, you will have an important tool for visualizing the person you want to be living the life you want to live.

I hope that what you take away from this chapter is the importance of finding your inner child again, of recapturing your ability to dream. To be successful, you need to be able close your eyes and *see* yourself getting that $10,000 commission or bonus check and *feel* the way you will feel when you get it. See yourself taking that vacation and feel yourself getting drinks on the beach. Now is the time to visualize the great moments to come! Visualize your future and begin to connect that excitement with the successful moments you have already experienced—and then put in the work to make those visualizations real!

FIND THE RIGHT MENTOR

Get comfortable asking the questions that you want answers to. Many times, we are afraid to approach people or network with people who are living the life we want to live. That makes no sense. Who could possibly know more about how to get from where you are to where they are than them? If you are to get the information you need to be a success, you need to get comfortable rubbing shoulders with people who are in the space you want to be in.

Principle Seven: Find a Mentor

No matter who you are, if you are cut, you will bleed red. It doesn't matter if you are black or white; man or woman; rich or poor. The only difference between a person who is successful and a person who is unsuccessful is successful people have the ability to turn thinking into action. One of the ways that I learned to put my own ideas into practice was by watching others do it. By watching what people were doing I was able to learn valuable skills and a mindset that helped push me forward. Look, life is full of ups and downs, but people on a path of success have principles that they live by. If you want to be successful, it is your job is to find what those principles are.

Here are some of the Key Principles I identified in successful people and that you should look for in a mentor:
Sometimes a mentor isn't always a boss.

Someone I considered a mentor is a gentlemen I mentioned earlier in the book the name of Mike Lerch he inspired me to always keep going and he wasn't afraid to share his dreams I learned many things from him. He shared with me about his dream of owning multiple buildings and apartment complexes his dream home. Funny thing is I have known this man for 13 years now in Oct and can I tell you he has accomplished 90% of his goals above. To find a great mentor you really only need to ask yourself do I want to be like him or her in 10 years. If the answer is yes than you might have the right person to plug into.

Make sure they keep their word to others

When you do what you say you're going to do, you build self-respect and a positive identity.

Make sure they understand that "failure" is feedback

When failure no longer makes you angry or insecure, it becomes something you can learn and grow from.

Make sure they have a vision

When you have a game plan, it becomes possible to map your way from where you to where you want to be.

Make sure they are passionate

Make sure they have a why

It is very important to find the right mentor, but how do you get someone to mentor you? The answer is much more straightforward than you might think: simply ask. Go up to a person who has the above qualities and say, "I am looking for guidance in my industry. Would you be willing to mentor me to get to the next level of my career?" If the answer is "yes," then you have found a mentor. If the answer is "no" then it is up to you not to let rejection stop your success.

As you grow, you may find that you have outgrown your mentor, that they are no longer in a position to give you help or guidance. That is okay—it means that you are moving in the right direction in life. A mentorship is not like marriage, it is mean to be temporary. Understand that you need to learn as much from your mentor as he or she is willing to teach. Once you have outgrown your mentor you should strive to maintain the relationship, but you needn't expect the relationship to last a lifetime.

Principle Eight: Be a Sponge

Your mentor is full of knowledge and information—soak it all up and then put it to use. Take notes to reference later on—it's important you review the things you learn from your mentor. Take notes bot only of what your mentor says, but also write down their daily habits. You never know what small things in their lives have big impacts on their success—and could do the same for you.

BUILD THE RIGHT RELATIONSHIPS

Build relationships one at a time

Building relationships comes easy for some people but is much more difficult for others. Regardless of whether you are great with people or not, this chapter is going to teach you how to build and maintain strong relationships with the people you are doing business with.

Principle Nine: Find Common Ground

Each time you have an interaction with someone, take a moment to find common ground with them. If your interaction is over the phone, listen closely and ask a few personal questions before getting down to business. Let them know that you take an interest in them as a person, not just as a customer. Ask about how their day was, or if they have any weekend plans? Taking a moment to appreciate someone can be very beneficial in many ways. For example I worked with a few people who had low self-steam and they beat themselves up whenever they did something wrong because they were so hard on themselves I begin to show them all the things they were doing right and can I tell you once I begin to help them change the conversation in there own head they begin to increase sales and they begin walking differently talking differently. People often ask me if this is some form of manipulation. It isn't even if asking these questions might benefit me in some way, I am genuinely interested in the answers and the people I am asking them of.

Principle Ten: Ask the Right Questions

Here is a list of questions to get people talking about them themselves (don't forget to give their answers your undivided attention).

Do you travel much for work?
Do you plan on going to the [insert name] conference?
Do you follow [insert local sports team's name]?
I see on your LinkedIn profile you went to [insert school
    name].

Don't just ask questions, tell people about yourself. Accept people the way they are. Assume that other people want to form relationships, too. Be friendly and show a genuine interest in the people around you. To do this, you may need to overcome your fear of rejection. It's important to realize that rejection will happen no matter what—it's a fact—but I have learned to take rejection with a smile, and you should try to do so as well.

ENJOY THE CHALLENGE

Realize that it is okay to be challenged in life but let yourself be motivated by those challenges rather than discouraged. It is okay to be frustrated, to have setbacks. Life is going to happen, and you are going fail, but that doesn't mean you can't enjoy those difficult moments. I am sure you are reading this and saying to yourself, *RAJ must be crazy! He expects me to enjoy my failures and setbacks?* I am not crazy at all. Getting to the point where you can take pleasure in your failures—because you know you will learn from them—is a clear sign that you are on track to get to the next level in your life.

Principle Eleven: Write Down All Your Challenges

In order to overcome the challenges that you face, you first need to know what they are. The best way to track your challenges is to write them all down. Only once you can see your challenges in front of you in black and white can you come up with creative ways to overcome them. That doesn't mean that you should dwell on the challenges you face. It is possible, after all, to focus so much on the issues preventing us from achieving our goals that we forget to focus on their solutions—and that can have a deleterious affect on our ability to perform at our peak.

There was a time when I was dealing with death in my family as well as a painful separation from the people I loved. In addition, around this time, I also had to admit a family member to a sober living facility and had a very difficult relationship with a business partner. I didn't let any of that stop me. No matter how tough it got, I didn't let it stop my progress—I kept rising. I believed it would get better, and it did. Part of the reason for my ability to persevere through this difficult time was that I began to make lists of the things that challenged me and made plans to overcome them. Life can get hard, and you *will* face challenges, but I am living proof that you can overcome anything that life throws in your path.

Principle Twelve: Rise to the Challenge

When challenged arise, too many people just give up. It's ok to feel upset or get frustrated when nothing seems to be going your way, but you cannot allow frustration to get the best of you. Challenges will come, it is up to you to maintain ep your peace. A good way to do this is to write out how you are going to solve those issues or visualize yourself solving those issues. Also, something that most people won't tell you is that if you don't have a solution to an issue then it's not your issue to solve. You can't control everything, and you can't solve every problem, but you can control how you respond to difficult situations at work or in life. You choose whether or not you rise to life's challenges.

Principle Thirteen: Get Help When You Need Help

For some reason, as we grow from children into men and women, we become afraid to ask for help. Don't be afraid to ask for help or information from people! Don't let one bad encounter asking for help from the teacher back when you were in school discourage you from asking for the help you *need* now. Look to people who are doing well in the area you are struggling in on. Ask a supervisor, a mentor, or a colleague. Don't be afraid. Ask.

Principal Fourteen: You Are Not Alone

Always remember that when you are going through challenges, others are going through similar challenges as well. What you are facing is not special or unique. When you do overcome life's challenges, be mindful; it is important to help others who are in a similar position to the one you were in. Any time that you are in a position to help another person, do not hesitate—help them. The love and compassion you show on your journey will be returned to you from others as you continue to grow in your life.

While you are challenged to grow, become smarter by reading, become healthier, and become more disciplined with your spending. All of your goals are right there within you reach if you put your research into action, and if you remain consistent—the subject of our next chapter.

CONSISTENCY

Now that you have read through this book, you should have a better understanding of the principles that will help bring you success. So many people will start a business a new job a hobby a sport or schooling when things get difficult over time people tend to lose faith when they don't see immediate results. Some people will even start a business hobby schooling etc and get results only to stop doing what it was that had brought them success and forget about all the steps they had to take to get them there. Before long, they are right back at square one. What stopped them from continuing on to even greater success is the focus of this final chapter: consistency.

Principle Fifteen: Write Out Three Quarterly Goals

Take the time to figure out three things you want to accomplish at work in the coming quarter a few days before the close of the current quarter—whether that be income-related or accolades you want to receive—and then write them down. Once your goals have been written down, read over them and visualize them in every possible way. That means thinking about not only what it will feel like to hit them, but all the steps it will take to get you there. If you can feel your dreams as if they have already happened, I know you will accomplish the unexpected.

Principle Sixteen: Create a Schedule for Yourself

Successful people plan their time! You can't win at everything, but most people who don't organize their time lose much more often than they win! What has always been helpful for me is to break my day into four quarters, so each day almost mirrors the sales cycle itself. Here is an example of how that would look in the real world: If you work at a call center and you want to make six figures this year, you need to make a total—including salary—of $25,000 or more in the first quarter. The daily habits that you create need to line up to meet this goal. So, if you need to call 125 people every single day to make an average of $300 in daily commission, then use those numbers to help you figure out how much work you need to be doing each hour of the business day. To help yourself stay on track, place reminders around your home and your workspace. Way too often, we forget "why" we want to accomplish these goals. Why is it that you are working hard? Why do you get up early every single day? Why do put up with what I do? Why do I keep doing what I am doing and see limited results? These are questions only you can answer.

Principle Seventeen: Make Promises Only if You Can Keep Them

Don't promise yourself the world when you know you can't deliver. What I mean is don't promise yourself that you will make a million dollars in commission in your first year at a new job. Not only is that an unrealistic goal, but not hitting it—and like not hitting it by a huge margin—could prove ultimately demotivating. I know I have been telling you to dream big throughout this book, and I do want you to do just that. However, I am also saying that success is a process—and sometimes a long one. If you want millions you need to learn to acquire thousands first.

Principle Eighteen: Reward Yourself When You Get Something Done

Learn to treat yourself and reward yourself for hitting your goals. If you set a target and met it, it is important that you mark that moment. While it is important to never lose site of the big picture and your big dreams, that does not mean that you can't pause to reward yourself for all that you have done. It is important not to reward yourself too much or too extravagantly, but it is equally important to celebrate each and every success. As you grow and learn how to manage this process—that is, as you grow more and more successful—you will find a way to live on roughly 50 – 60% of your income while investing and banking the rest.

CLOSING

This book has been my attempt to share all the things I have learned along my path from broke teenage father to successful man. If you would like a customized Game Plan or ideas on how to visualize your success go to my website www.guptavision.com and connect with me so that I can help you on a more personal level. I know you can take the information in this book and grow as I did. Soon, you will see results. More importantly, though, you will continue to grow as a person. This journey isn't as easy one, but I am positive that no matter where you are in life, you can change and improve your life—your destiny is in *your* hands.

I would not have made it to where I am without the help, mentorship, friendship, and love of other people. Under the mentorship of Mike Lerch, Mike Lowery, Nate Brush and Wesly Danniels. I learned not only about management and sales techniques, but about how to live my life and be a good person. Julisa Hernadez is one of the strongest, most passionate, fearless, beautiful, and loving women I have met. I began to manage her professionally in August 2009. It didn't take long for us to forge a meaningful friendship outside of the office.

Soon, she was a trusted friend and advisor; later my wife and the mother of our two beautiful children. I wouldn't be the man I am today without her patience and support. We have been through a lot over the years, and I couldn't have done what I have done without her. Thank you to my Grandparents Willie and Sandra fletcher they have been a rock over the years and my parents I love you all and thank you.

Printed in the United States
By Bookmasters